# These Dandelion Days



Ela Yanik

BookLeaf Publishing

Presentation by *BookLeaf Publishing*

Web: www.bookleafpub.com

E-mail: info@bookleafpub.com

ISBN: 9789357445924

First edition 2023

# PREFACE

"Trying to save the youth without putting your shoes on"
- Alex Turner, It's Hard To Get Around the Wind

# home

Lavender trees
Lavender feelings
Whisper,
You're home.

'Let's go outside',
To feel dazed
Sunlight bounce
And joy,

Twirl among the sunbeams
Of white among blue,

A ride.
Down and far and fast
With the waves of the wind,
Strokes of waves
Among your dainty skin
Bare and free,

Meeting the river,
Leading to nowhere
Leading to everywhere,

Laughs and cries.

We must go back,
Everything is temporary.

Now my lavender tree,
Placed in a ceramic vase
By the window,
Closed,
Looking out to where it truly wants to be.

# moon

These ongoing attempts
Of counting every star in a light-polluted city
Are, undoubtedly,
Useless endeavours.

And so now,
All I do is count the moon,
Feeling content with knowing
That the simplest of tasks,
Are always enough.

# puddles

Leave the passenger seat
Just to walk along the motorway,
Tissue paper boots
And deep puddles of youth.

The sunflower on my skin
Seems to fade faster in this rainstorm.

Was I always this naive?
Maybe.

Let's cure it with experience.

# friends at breakfast

This perfect pairing
Of apple and cinnamon,
Sunday morning, and
Flower chain of conversation
Decorating the breakfast table.

Connecting the dots
Of photobooth memories,
Finding laughter in the disaster
Of the night before, only to
Play that one song and sing, effortlessly.

Questioning our sobriety,
We pour the tea
Sharing envelope feelings
And deep ambitions,
Vulnerable souls in complete comfort,
Navigating life
And womanhood
Together.

# reality

Modern world of abundance
In which I add this tally of twenty
Yet why, do these cycles around the sun
Seem denser in fear each year,

Left alone,
And learning to swim for the first time
In this pacific sea of possibilities,
Newspaper lifejackets with broken promises
Smudging black into blue,

Joining queues of no beginning
For the rat race of life,
The prize?
Trophy of dust and wasted time.

Wired headphones
In an age of disconnection,
I take a walk.
Useless,
But absolutely necessary.

# those days

You know those days
When your reflection is strange,
And the weather unkind.
Weighted ceilings and tasteless coffee,
Bathing in unwelcome feelings
That flood the room and stain the walls.
An unescapable idleness
Buried under unwashed clothes.

Hair feels lifeless,
Life feels pointless.

Those days
I know.

# 2am

It's 2am.
Yet with you,
I still feel sunlight.

# night of youth

This endless ninth cloud,
Arriving on these limitless streets
Which vein this small town
We now call home.

November cold immunity
And radio fever,
Fuelling our euphoric freedom
Seemingly eternal.

These misguided delights
Written in our salad days,
Spilling drink on my white shirt
And stumbling in the road

To dance
Make noise and laughter
Upon this silently spinning earth,

Mellow drama.
A regretful kiss.
Worries,

But only fleeting,
As we exist in mutual assurance

That it will all be okay.
One day

# cold tea

I let the cookies burn
And the tea go cold.
I let the sad song play
And the rose grow old.

I let the rain inside
Leave the door slightly open.
I let these things happen
In times of feeling broken.

# an evening with you

Today we are together
Over the dining table,

Light your favourite candle and
Remove the outside darkness,
A flicker
And we're warm.

Intimate discussions
Once unmentionable
Now mentioned.
Red at your questions,
Pale at your answers,

Careless flow,
The bottle emptier
And soon empty in a
Growing room of stories,

Tuck me in
Tight and cosy and safe,
Reassure me
Through books of fiction,
Peck on the head
And a warm goodnight.

Remember those days,
That love stays.

Now,
Feeling comfort in your intimate stories,
Seeing safety in the soft blue of your eyes.
My tears are yours,
As yours mine, likewise.

# dreamer

To be a dreamer,
Is to be
A liar.

And so I will,
Be exactly that.

A living contradiction.

# dandelion days

These are my dandelion days,
Whisked away by this careful breeze
To unknowing destinations
Meeting earth's many corners,
And many edges,
Float among deep horizons
Between magic and dust,

Caught in a branch,
But only for a moment, then

Delicate landing on the grass
In a meadow of colour
Green and pure, only
Growing, growing, growing,

Blooming,
And bloomed.
New version of the very same.

Only to be whisked away again.

# fragile

My body of glass.
Loose grip,
Only to fall
And shatter.

Release the flood,
And start again.

# coffee shop

We meet in a coffee shop
Around the corner of our youth.
Brisk welcome, glance and embrace.
Smell of experiences.
Different but the same.

What's new
With you?

Life has changed.
Isn't it great.

# a good day

A blanket of blue sky
Comforting this bustling city,
Drying out the anxieties
Embedded in the floor as wet rain
That visited the night before.

Take a walk among clear paths,
Nourishing laughter
And a sip of sweet coffee,

With little birds
Upon wooden fences,
And little stories
To keep us company,

Flower markets of
Strawberry red and
Sunlight yellows,
Meeting raw light of bliss.

Feather-like feelings
Floating among this delicate air,
My thoughts cloudless,
Comforted by the goodness
Of these effortless joys that made today,
Today.

# systems

Abundance of plastic buckets
In a diamond rainstorm
Never-ending.

This broken cycle,
Decaying fields,
And the hungry.
A permanent mark in our earth.
A system that pollutes.

Go back to the days
Of catching rain in our palms
Just to wash our faces.

# sun

We all have a sun,
To wrap and keep for later,
Tight grip for when the days
Seem too dark
For too long.

Find yours,
Keep it close.

# window seat

Window seat
Gaze and contemplation,
Head against the glass,
Who really am I?

A privilege to be no one
But a passenger
Among passengers
Onboard a train flowing in motion,
Nameless for a moment in time.

From city to city,
Through fields and forests,
Interconnectedness exists in the most sublime
And in the simplest of ways,
As life connects life, with

One more story to tell
Only leading to another,
And another and another

In a seemingly ceaseless construction
Of this bridge of opportunities
In what we call living.

The final destination
But still,
I do not know myself.

And thankfully so, as
Life is still in motion
And I don't want to get off.
Not for a while.

www.ingramcontent.com/pod-product-compliance
Lightning Source LLC
Chambersburg PA
CBHW051720130826
49812CB00034B/1273
*9789357445924*